Mel Bay Presents Stefan Grossman's Guitar Workshop Audio Series

Masterpieces of Country Blues Guitar

from the playing of Blind Blake, Bo Carter,
Scrapper Blackwell, Rev. Gary Davis, Blind Boy Fuller,
Tommy Johnson, Big Bill Broonzy and Josh White

taught by Woody Mann

Contents

1 2 3 4 5 6 7 8 9 0

Weeping Willow
Blind Boy Fuller

3

Policy Blues
Bo Carter

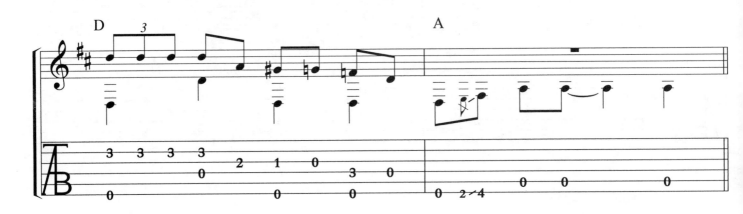

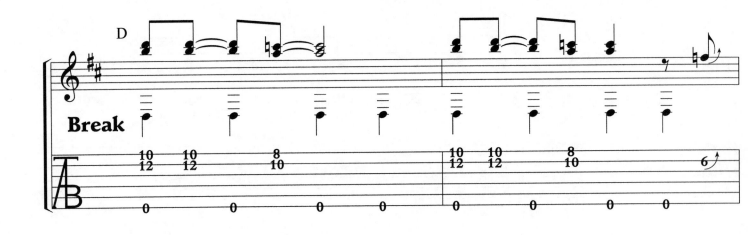

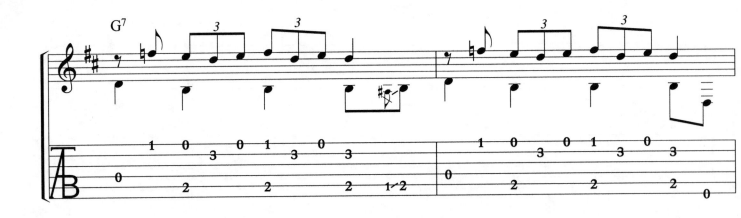

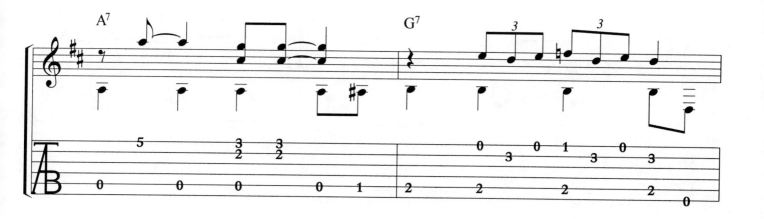

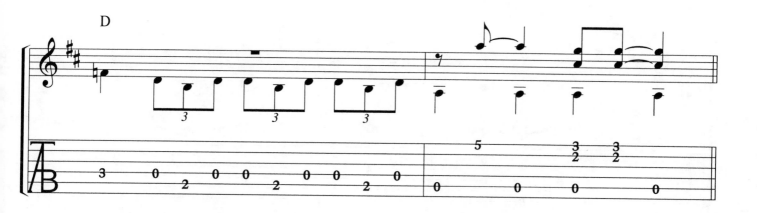

Verse Variation

8

Bye Bye Blues
Tommy Johnson

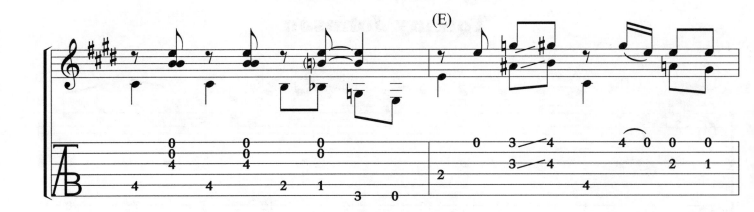

(E)

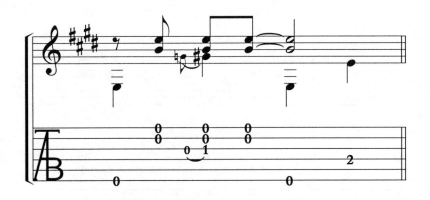

Alternate Bar 4

Alternate Bar 10

Sylvester Weaver & Sara Martin

Long Tall Mama
Big Bill Broonzy

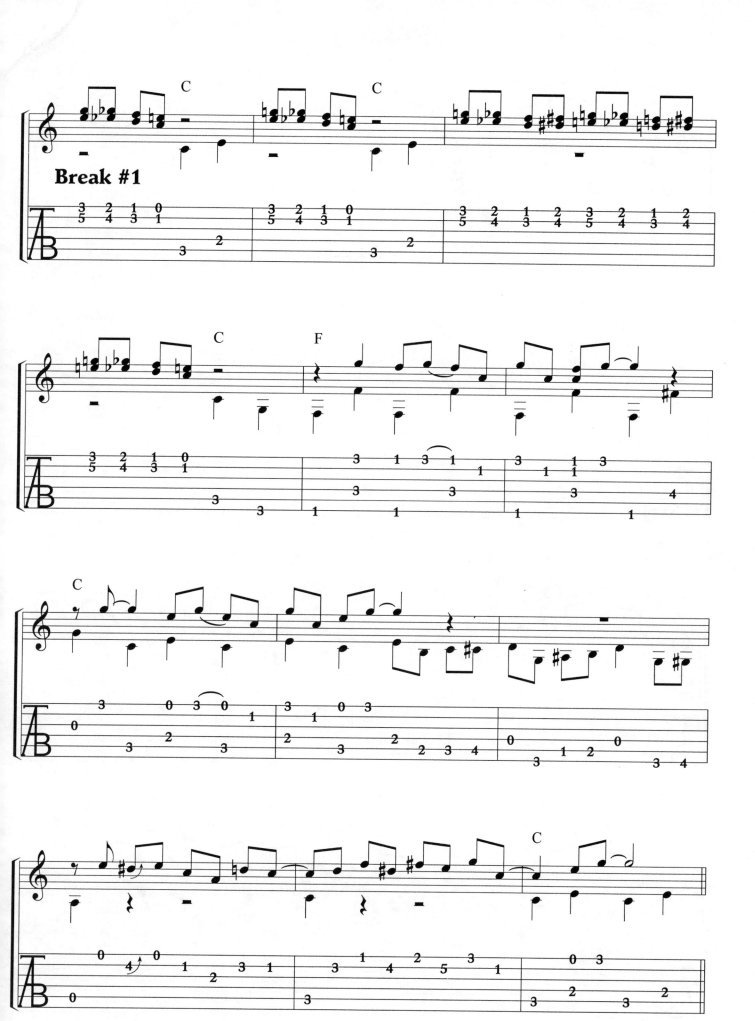

Break #1

13

Break #2

14

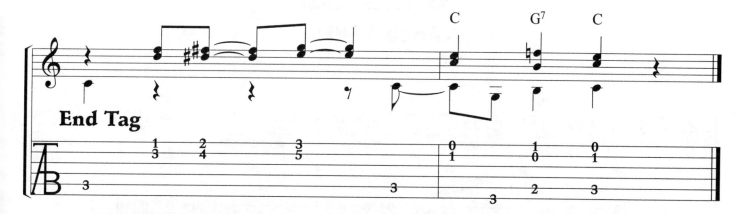

End Tag

Big Bill Broonzy

Good Gal
Josh White

Open D Tuning: DADF#AD

Josh White

Kokomo Blues
Scrapper Blackwell

19

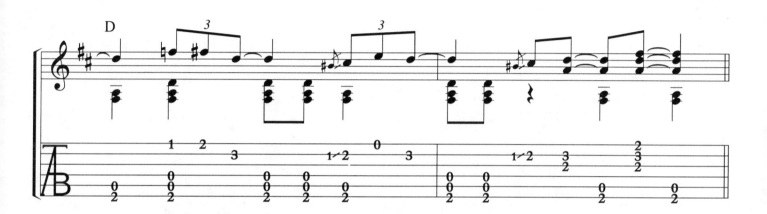

Scrapper Blackwell

Chump Man Blues
Blind Blake

Drop D Tuning: DADGBE

Blind Blake

Southern Rag
Blind Blake

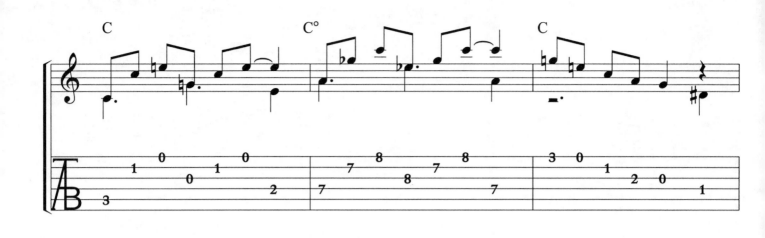

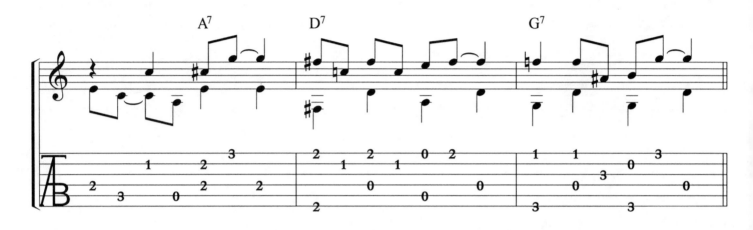

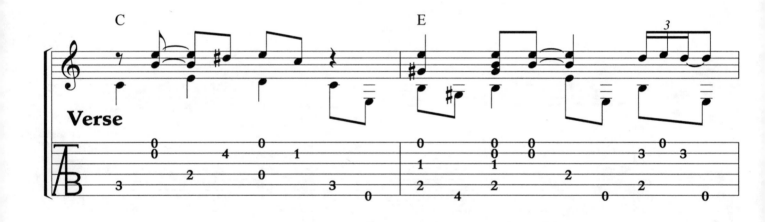

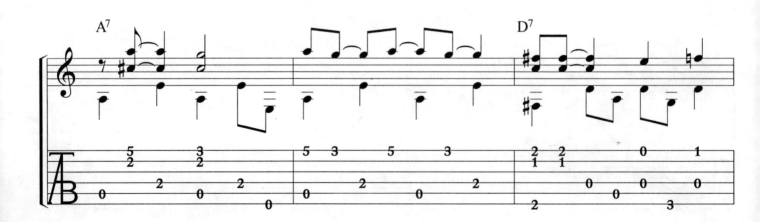

Buddy Moss playing guitar in prison

Oh Glory How Happy I Am
Rev. Gary Davis

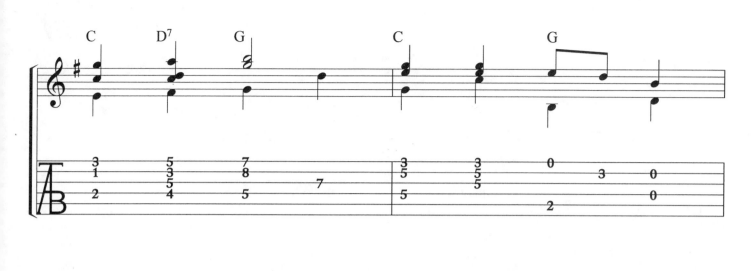

(Syncopated)

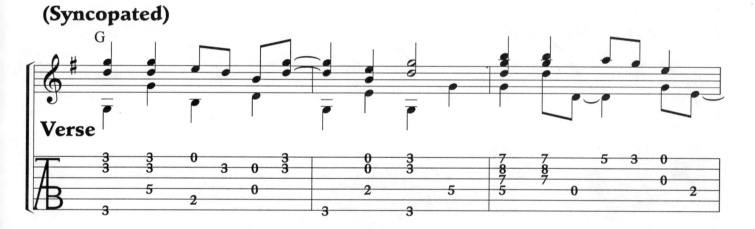

Verse

Chorus

Rev. Gary Davis

CD Track Listings

The audio lessons in this series were originally recorded in the 1970s. They were initially released on audio cassettes. We have gone back to our master tapes to get the best possible sound for this new CD edition. Certain references to albums that are no longer available or information that is out of date have been edited out. These lessons originally came with different print material. These were handwritten and in some cases offered only tab transcriptions. The lessons have now been typeset in tab/music. As a result some spoken references on the CDs regarding page numbers or a position of a line or phrase on a page may differ slightly from the written tab/music in this new edition. We have annotated as carefully and exactly as possible what each track on the CDs present. Please use these track descriptions as your reference guide.

Lesson One

Track 1: Blind Boy Fuller performs *Weeping Willow*
Track 2: Woody performs *Weeping Willow*
Track 3: Introduction to lesson
Track 4: Tuning
Track 5: Teaching of first two bars of *Weeping Willow*
Track 6: Playing of first two bars and teaching of third to sixth bars
Track 7: Playing of fifth and sixth bars and teaching of seventh bar
Track 8: Teaching of bars eight to twelve
Track 9: Playing of bars ten to twelve
Track 10: *Weeping Willow* played slowly
Track 11: *Weeping Willow* played faster
Track 12: *Weeping Willow* played with syncopation
Track 13: Closing thoughts and further discussion on picking technique
Track 14: Woody performs *Weeping Willow*
Track 15: Bo Carter performs *Policy Blues*
Track 16: *Woody performs Policy Blues*
Track 17: Introduction to *Policy Blues*
Track 18: Playing of introduction
Track 19: Teaching of introduction
Track 20: Playing of introduction
Track 21: Teaching of Verse
Track 22: Verse played slowly
Track 23: Verse played faster

Track 24: Teaching of first two bars of Break
Track 25: Playing of first two bars of Break
Track 26: Teaching of third and fourth bars of Break
Track 27: Playing of third and fourth bars of Break
Track 28: Teaching of fifth to twelfth bars of Break
Track 29: Break played slowly
Track 30: Some additional thoughts and techniques
Track 31: Break played a little faster
Track 32: Complete arrangement played
Track 33: Closing thoughts on *Policy Blues*
Track 34: *Policy Blues* played from top with different syncopations
Track 35: Tommy Johnson performs *Bye Bye Blues*
Track 36: Woody performs *Bye Bye Blues*
Track 37: Introduction to tune
Track 38: Teaching of first two bars
Track 39: Playing of first two bars
Track 40: Teaching of third to ninth bars
Track 41: Playing of third to ninth bars
Track 42: Teaching of tenth and eleventh bars
Track 43: Playing of tenth and eleventh bars with alternate tenth bar
Track 44: Closing thoughts on *Bye Bye Blues*
Track 45: Playing of *Bye Bye Blues* as written and then using different brush strokes

Lesson Two

Track 1: Big Bill Broonzy performs *Long Tall Mama*
Track 2: Woody performs *Long Tall Mama*
Track 3: Introduction to lesson
Track 4: Tuning
Track 5: Teaching of verse
Track 6: Verse played slowly
Track 7: Verse played faster
Track 8: Teaching of bars thirteen to twenty-one of First Break
Track 9: Playing of bars nineteen to twenty-four of First Break
Track 10: Teaching of bars twenty-two to twenty-four of First Break
Track 11: Playing of bars twenty-one to twenty-four of First Break
Track 12: Playing of First Break
Track 13: Teaching of bars twenty-five to thirty-five of Second Break
Track 14: Playing of bars thirty-two to thirty-five of Second Break
Track 15: Teaching of End Tag
Track 16: Playing of both Breaks slowly
Track 17: Teaching of alternating thumb and finger for single note runs
Track 18: Playing of complete arrangement
Track 19: Josh White performs *Good Gal*
Track 20: Woody performs *Good Gal*
Track 21: Introduction to tune
Track 22: Tuning to Open D Tuning
Track 23: Teaching of chord positions in Open D Tuning
Track 24: Teaching of first two bars
Track 25: Playing of first two bars slowly
Track 26: Teaching of third to sixth bars
Track 27: Playing of fifth and sixth bars
Track 28: Teaching of seventh to tenth bars

Track 29: Playing of ninth and tenth bars
Track 30: Teaching of eleventh and twelfth bars
Track 31: Playing of *Good Gal* slowly
Track 32: Playing of *Good Gal* faster
Track 33: Scrapper Blackwell performs *Kokomo Blues*
Track 34: Woody performs *Kokomo Blues*
Track 35: Discussion of Scrapper Blackwell's techniques
Track 36: Playing of Introduction
Track 37: Teaching of first two bars
Track 38: Playing of first two bars
Track 39: Teaching of third and fourth bars
Track 40: Playing of third to fifth bars
Track 41: Teaching of fifth bar of Introduction
Track 42: Playing of Introduction
Track 43: Teaching first bar of Verse
Track 44: Playing of first two bars of Verse
Track 45: Teaching of third and fourth bars of Verse
Track 46: Playing of third and fourth bars of Verse
Track 47: Teaching of fifth to tenth bars of Verse
Track 48: Playing of ninth and tenth bars of Verse
Track 49: Teaching of eleventh and twelfth bars of Verse
Track 50: Playing of Verse slowly
Track 51: Playing of Verse with Snapping Technique and Dampening
Track 52: Teaching of Bending Technique
Track 53: Teaching of Alternate seventh and eighth bars of Verse
Track 54: Plays Alternate seventh and eighth bars of Verse
Track 55: Playing of Verse with Alternate seventh and eighth bars
Track 56: Closing thoughts

Lesson Three

Track 1: Blind Blake performs *Chump Man Blues*
Track 2: Woody performs *Chump Man Blues*
Track 3: Introduction to lesson
Track 4: Tuning
Track 5: Teaching of first two bars and rhythmic pattern
Track 6: Playing of first bar
Track 7: Playing of first two bars
Track 8: Teaching of third to twelfth bars
Track 9: Playing *Chump Man Blues* slowly
Track 10: Teaching of alternate tenth bar
Track 11: Playing of ninth to twelfth bars using alternate tenth bar
Track 12: Playing of *Chump Man Blues* using alternate tenth bar
Track 13: Discussion about adding more double thumbing
Track 14: Playing of *Chump Man Blues* adding more double thumbing
Track 15: Discussion of combining different blues techniques
Track 16: Blind Blake performs *Southern Rag*
Track 17: Woody performs *Southern Rag*
Track 18: Introduction to *Southern Rag*
Track 19: Teaching of a typical Blind Blake riff (seventeenth and eighteenth bars)
Track 20: Playing of seventeenth and eighteenth bars
Track 21: Teaching of Introduction
Track 22: Playing of Introduction

Track 23: Playing of Introduction faster
Track 24: Teaching of Verse
Track 25: Playing of Verse
Track 26: Continuing of teaching
Track 27: Playing of Introduction and Verse
Track 28: Woody performs *O'Glory How Happy I Am*
Track 29: Introduction to *O'Glory How Happy I Am*
Track 30: Tuning
Track 31: Discussion on brushing the bass
Track 32: Teaching of first two bars
Track 33: Playing of first two bars
Track 34: Teaching of third and fourth bars
Track 35: Playing of third and fourth bars
Track 36: Teaching of fifth bar
Track 37: Playing fifth and sixth bars
Track 38: Teaching of seventh and eighth bars
Track 39: Playing of first eight bars
Track 40: Teaching of first two bars of the Chorus
Track 41: Playing of first two bars of the Chorus
Track 42: Playing of Verse and Chorus
Track 43: Closing thoughts
Track 44: Playing *O'Glory How Happy I Am* with syncopation